# Shattering the Glass Walls
## Of the
## Woman in Ministry

By

Cheryl Turnbull

© *Copyright 2008 Cheryl Turnbull. All rights reserved.*
*ISBN: 978-0-615-26294-9*

*No part of this book may be reproduced, stored in a retrieval system, or transmitted by any means without the written permission of the author.*

*Printed in the United States of America.*

*This book is printed on acid-free paper.*

## Contents

Acknowledgements - 7

Introduction - 9

Chapter One - 11
God's Gals: Charmin Covered Brillo Women

Chapter Two - 21
God's Gals: Confident and Compassionate Cuties

Chapter Three - 29
God's Gals: Called to Serve

Chapter Four - 39
God's Gals: The Ezer Kenegdo Woman

Chapter Five - 47
God's Gals: Discovering Her Priorities

Chapter Six - 55
God's Gals: Having Fun with Who She is

Chapter Seven - 65
God's Gals: Avoiding Burnout

Chapter Eight - 73
God's Gals: Romancing Her Man

Chapter Nine - 83
God's Gals: Rediscovering Ministry

Chapter Ten - 97
God's Gals: Celebrating the Fulfilled Life

Suggested Reads - 103

About the Author - 105

## *Acknowledgements*

First, I want to thank God for His grace and mercy. Without His loving hand, gently loving me, I would never have put my thoughts to paper. I thank Him every day for His goodness.

I want to thank my very loving husband for the support he has given me while putting this book together. If he were not behind me in this endeavor, I could not have completed the project. We have come through much, and have become closer, developing a stronger relationship through it all. Thank you Sweetheart, I love you.

I also want to thank my children, Jonathan, Daniel, Christina, and Catherine. They had to transition with us, and it was not easy. They are all great fighters and I appreciate the fight they have within them, to combat Satan's attacks against our family. I believe we are all stronger, because of it. Please always remember; "God will get you through, anything; even if it seems He is not listening. He loves you and will be there for you, when you are ready."

To my parents, Gerald and Peggy Johnson, I want to say a

big thank you for raising me in the faith; giving me the foundation I needed for a life of ministry. You are great prayer warriors and I thank you for those prayers.

The faith, prayers, and support of my husband's parents, Reverends Robert and Arleta Turnbull, have been a tremendous blessing, throughout the years of our ministry. Through the ups and downs they have been right behind us in prayer. Thank you so much for all you have done for our family.

Thank you Larry Hickey, the Assemblies of God Potomac District Superintendent and Linda Webb, the Assemblies of God Potomac District Director of Women's Ministries for the support and encouragement as I developed this entire project. It meant a lot to me, to have your support in getting this "off and running."

## *Introduction*

When I started on my journey as the wife of a youth pastor twenty-six years ago, there was no training on what a woman was to expect from her role as the wife of a pastor. We had to learn as we went and "grin and bear it."

For the generation before me it was ok to live that way. My generation is in the between stage of knowing it needs to change and wondering what to do. This generation wants to "know our story." They want to know where we've been and how it's done…"the good, the bad, and the ugly."

There are too many ministers and their wives leaving ministry, due to the stress and strain the pastorate puts on their family. The women of today's generation want to know how ministry is done and what is expected of them. Just what does it mean to be the wife of a pastor or woman in ministry? We need to share with them and show them what it means to take our family with us in ministry, without losing them to the world.

It is my heart's desire to help cultivate strong relationships between women in ministry and the wives of pastors. My passion is to be a person that influences the generations into a strong relationship with God and a passion to see His Word taken to the nations. We have the privilege of being called by God to share His love and mercy with the people around us and support the men in our lives.

My prayer is that as you read this book you will be encouraged and refueled to go just a little bit farther; to be tough and hang in there, and take your children with you on the adventure of ministry. Not all women have been chosen by God to do what we do. God chose each one of you wonderful women because He knew you would have the determination to fulfill the call. As you read let your soul be healed and restored, or just be encouraged that there are others, just like you, feeling just as you feel.

Blessings to you as you read.

## Chapter One

### Charmin covered Brillo Woman
*Being tough enough to take life as it comes at you, Keeping your heart soft in the process*

**Recognizing and Surviving the Cost of Ministry**

A brillo pad is used to clean those tough pots and pans that ordinary sponges cannot get clean. The Holy Spirit cleans our life like a brillo pad, getting the hard things in our heart out that we cannot do on our own. During this process God helps our heart stay soft to the touch. I want you to ask yourself the following questions and be honest in your answers.

Is being called worth the cost?
Why?
Is being called truly a privilege?
Why?
In this chapter it is my desire to get across that, "YES," it is worth it and "YES," it is a privilege to be called by God into ministry.

There are many ups and downs to this life of ministry. It is totally up to us how we deal with and handle them. We can let our spiritual life suffer, by letting hurt turn into anger. Anger, if not dealt with will eventually turn into bitterness. Or, we can allow the Holy Spirit to mature us to new, higher levels in Him. *"In your anger do not sin: Do not let the sun go down while you are still angry, and do not give the devil a foothold."* Eph. 4:26, 27 NIV

### *Responding Successfully to the Ministry Challenge*

What do we do when we are hurt? Do we lash out? Do we hold it inside? How we react to the hurts and disappointments in ministry and our life will affect us positively or negatively. We have two choices: one choice is to let God mature our spirit, the other choice is to let our enemy, the devil, destroy our spirit and eventually our life.

Dr. Chris Thurman in his book, *"The Lies We Believe,"* says, *"Most of our unhappiness and emotional struggles are caused by the lies we tell ourselves."* He goes on to say that until we recognize these lies and replace them with truth emotional health is impossible. (pg 22)

I didn't realize it at the time, but I let hurts from our first pastorate, issues in two of our churches, and the disappointment of our handicapped son fester in my heart throughout years of ministry. Even though I had been around positive preachers, I was unknowingly letting these negative issues affect my spirit and thoughts.

All around us we are told by the media, by women, by the law, and even by some churches that we don't have to put up with this; we can get out of the situation if we choose. I had let all the hurts and disappointments culminate to the point of despair in my life. I didn't hear the voice of truth, because by the time I reached the point of despair, I had made up my mind and didn't want to hear the truth. I was not looking to the Source; I was looking at *things* in my life God had not answered.

The reality was I was looking at lies and listening to Satan's words, not God's. I had to admit and confess all my wrong thinking. I had to ask God to forgive me and get me back on track. I would not wish that point of desperation on anyone.

You might be wondering how I could let myself get to that point. In all honesty I needed to be truthful with myself. I needed someone else to help me see that the road I was taking was only leading to destruction. I needed another woman in ministry, but I did not have that kind of a friendship.

## *The Power of Godly Friendships*

We can have another woman as a friend outside of ministry, but they will not understand some of the issues relating to the pastorate. In fact, they may influence us in the wrong direction. We do not want to get to the state of mind in which I had allowed myself to reach. That is the reason for *"Mentoring Women in Ministry."*

It is my heart's desire to help cultivate strong relationships; relationships with other women who are just like you, in the trenches, giving their lives for the work of the Lord. If you are able to meet once a month, for ten months, with other women do so, it will be a tremendous encouragement and support.

Make a very determined effort to not let the meeting become some superficial meeting once a month, in which you are not open and cannot share. Let the goal of the ten month period make each of you stronger, closer, and more trusting of each other.

The meetings are not meant to be a time of bashing churches or spouses or blaming other people for hurts and disappointments. If there is hurt it is to be a time of healing. If it feels like you are spiritually dying it is to be a time of restoration. If you are just starting out in ministry or feel you are just fine, then it is to be a preventative maintenance regimen.

During the formative years in ministry it is exciting to see God use us. As I began ministry with my husband I worked with the choir as well as helped in the youth ministry.

However, our senior pastor was constantly telling my husband to make sure he controlled his wife (me) and didn't let her boss him around. The senior pastor's wife would tell me to do things to my husband I thought was not right, but I did it because of the respect I had for her position.

At the time the things she would tell me to do I thought were very degrading and very much like a mother telling a son what to do, not a husband. These things led to disagreements and struggles within our marriage. I let this get into my spirit without realizing it. It would fester there until years later.

I was not even aware this was happening. As women, we need to be very careful in what we allow to harbor in our hearts. It is so important to daily ask the Lord to cleanse our heart of any impurities and make sure we get rid of any doubt, hurt and misunderstandings. If they are not dealt with from the start they will be much harder to get rid of later. Do not disrespect the senior pastor's wife. Make sure you stay in the scripture and look for good mentors. Seek God for wisdom.

We have come such a long way from where we were when I started in ministry. There is definitely a move of God that is changing the culture of how we do life in the pastorate. If you are not in that type of a church atmosphere then here are some suggestions.

Find a friend in whom you can be accountable. Share your hurts and fears with her. Ask her to pray and make you responsible for your thoughts and feelings. Do not be fake and dishonest. Be real and open. That is the only way you are going to be able to overcome the anger and hurt.

Dr. Thurman, in *The Lies We Believe* quotes James Allen from his book *As A Man Thinketh*; "*Every thought seed sown or allowed to fall into the mind and to take root there produces its own kind. Good thoughts bear good fruit, bad thoughts bad."* (pg24)

Dr. Thurman points out that lies are beliefs, expectations, and attitudes that are not reality. We get these expectations and attitudes from a variety of places: i.e. media like TV, radio, magazines, movies, etc. Our culture tells us we are to look, act, and talk a certain way. Even in ministry there are certain ways we are suppose to act and dress or people will look at us strangely. I am not talking about what the Bible says regarding how to dress and act. I am talking about the culture of ministry.

When we attend church functions or denominational meetings what is going through our head? What do I wear? What will so and so be wearing? We are to look presentable. It is ok to want to look good, but do not get carried away. We do not want to make others feel less than perfect if they don't have what we have, or we should not feel bad if we can't afford what someone else has.

God will look at our heart.

He will give us exactly what we need.

What does our heart look like?

Is it happy in ministry or frustrated?

In our first position as youth pastors there were many good things that happened. My husband and I were able to form lasting relationships with the teenagers under our care as well as their parents. Several teens came to visit us in our church about two hours away, after they had grown up and married. Parents would visit and remind us of the good seeds we had sown in our first ministry.

In fact, we had been back in the area of our first youth pastorate for about three years. My husband was working on his doctorate and working as a chaplain in a local hospital nursing center. He received a phone call to perform the funeral service for a grandparent of some of the teens we ministered to twenty-five years earlier. They wanted me to sing a special song and lead a congregational song for the service. That was a sad time for them, but it was encouraging to know how much our lives had touched that family.

In the church in which we stayed for ten years my husband poured his heart into ministering to the flock, and I poured my heart into the youth ministry, led worship, and directed musical dramas. We look back on that ministry now and see God's hand in the lives of the people. Five of the youth in that church have gone on to become ministers in some form or another. There were tough times, but God used us in spite of our weaknesses. Doesn't the Bible say, "In our weakness He becomes strong?"

Take time right now to be open with yourself, if you are reading this alone, or with each other if you are meeting with other women. Think of the good things God is doing in your ministry. Sometimes we just need to remind ourselves, especially when we are down, of what God is doing. There is a saying that goes something like this, "when you feel you can't do anything and aren't worth much read your resume'," it will inspire you.

*Conclusion*

Let's answer the first two questions of this chapter.

Yes, it is worth the cost to be in ministry, and it is a privilege. God places a desire in our heart to spread His word. Each of us will have different ways of spreading His word, and we will discuss that in a later chapter. It is up to us what we make of the ministry. We have to make sure we are telling our self the truth and read our resumes, to remind us of our calling and accomplishments.

It would be great if you could find one other woman in ministry to partner with and share from the heart where you are right now. Share some hurts if you have any. Share some prayer needs. Share an encouraging word with each other. If you are reading this alone get a notebook to right down your thoughts. Keep it with this book so you can write down your thoughts as you read.

If you are meeting with others take a sheet of paper and fill it out with name, address, phone, email, birthday, anniversary, and spouse and children's names. Copy the paper for each woman so you will each have the opportunity to get to know more about one another and their families.

Pair up with a partner for a month. Touch base weekly either by email or phone. Become a prayer partner and confidant. Share what God is doing in your life and with your family. Let God begin to do some awesome works in each of you.

*My Thoughts and Notes*

## Chapter Two

## Confident and Compassionate Cuties
*Knowing who we are in Christ and caring for
those around us unconditionally
Phil. 1:6 and Col. 3:12-14*

**Attitude and Maturity Matters**

Pride and self-confidence without the Holy Spirit, lead to anger, resentment, and bitterness.

1 Samuel 15:2, 3, The Message, *"I'm about to get even with Amalek for ambushing Israel when Israel came up out of Egypt. Here's what you are to do. Go to war against Amalek. Put everything connected with Amalek under a holy ban. And no exceptions. This is to be total destruction – men and women, children and infants, cattle and sheep, camels and donkeys – the works!" vv 7-11 "Then Saul went after Amalek, from the canyon all the way to Shur near the Egyptian border. He captured Agag, king of Amalek, alive.*

*Everyone else was killed under the holy ban. Saul and the army made an exception for Agag, and for the choice sheep and cattle. They didn't include them under the terms of the holy ban. But all the rest, which nobody wanted anyway, they destroyed as decreed by the holy ban. Then God spoke to Samuel: 'I'm sorry I ever made Saul king. He's turned his back on me. He refuses to do what I tell him.'"*

Samuel goes on to remind Saul that he had nothing when he started out, then God made him head of Israel – made him king! What a privilege! *"God sent you off with orders. Why did you not obey Him? Why, with God's eyes on you all the time, did you brazenly carry out this evil?"(vv 17-19)* Saul starts making excuses and asks what is wrong with taking a few choice sheep? He was avoiding the issue.

That reminds me of one of my daughters when she was seventeen. She deliberately disobeyed and wrote me a long letter apologizing and explaining why she did what she did. She was making excuses. She missed the point of her deliberate disobedience.

Samuel told Saul straight up that he did not want sacrifices and empty rituals. He wanted him to listen and do what he told him. Because Saul refused to listen and said no to God, God said no to Saul's kingship.

In our own ministries we need to be careful not to become prideful in our accomplishments and knowledge, thinking we know more than anyone else. Too often I have seen young youth pastors or associates and their wives come into church all excited about ministry, but exemplify an attitude of, "I know more than you."

This is not healthy for them, or the church in which they are ministering. They will not be able to glean from the knowledge of those who have gone before them. I have seen wonderful ministries, such as *Master's Commission* or other similar programs, teach servant leadership. They teach students to develop a servant heart. The ministry teaches the student that all areas of the church give you an opportunity in which to minister, whether it be cleaning the bathrooms or speaking in front of a group of fifty or a thousand people. You learn that the attitude of the heart is important, not what special abilities you have.

There was an instance in one of our churches where my husband hired a part-time associate and his wife, to help with our worship and couples ministries. My husband and I wanted to help this man and his wife get back on their feet after coming from a difficult situation. I was the worship leader and music director at our church at the time.

In order to get a glimpse of the whole picture I am going to give a little background of where we were in our church. The church was very traditional when we first came and only had an organ and piano for worship. Over a period of five years we were able to add drums, bass and electric guitar, keyboard, viola as well as singers. We had a great band. It was exciting and new. People who visited the church were enjoying what was happening. The congregation loved where we were taking our worship. I felt a board member was influencing my husband's judgment on how worship should be handled. As I would lead and people were raising their hands in worship this man stood with his arms folded and a stern look on his face. Certain people in our church felt as if women should not be in a place of leadership. *I allowed* this to become a point of contention between my husband and me.

This couple who came to the church as part-time associates had a background in leading worship. I knew this, so I asked my husband to speak to them about becoming our worship leader. This would give me more time to devote to the youth ministry and I would not have to worry about the reaction of people to the way I lead worship. We took this young couple out for dinner, had them over to our house, and shared our vision of the church. As the senior pastor's wife I was excited to have another woman in ministry on board.

They must have not seen it that way. They never invited us over and never wanted to spend time with us. They had other couples over and spent time with them, but not us. They allowed others to voice complaints without stopping them. This is not a wise thing to do. If you are just starting out in ministry remember that God has placed the leaders in authority over you. If you are on board with a ministry support the senior pastor wholeheartedly. If you cannot do this it is better for you, the staff and the church if you leave. Leave without saying negative things about the pastor and do not take people from the congregation with you. God will honor that decision.

I am sure this couple had good intentions by showing the people they cared about what they thought, but more often than not it was meant to degrade the pastor and leadership. Remember it is a privilege to be in ministry, and Satan is trying his best to keep God's anointed from moving forward in their calling. One way in which he does this is by causing dissention among ministers and church members. Do not be deceived.

Now if you are a staff pastor the best way do deal with this situation is to tell the person making the complaint it would be best to go to the pastor and share with him their concerns. The pastor will hear the complaint directly from the source and try to come up with a solution. You should never listen to these complaints. You are only feeding negative thoughts into your spirit and that is not healthy.

This couple had the attitude of; "We know how to lead worship and raise kids better than anyone. No one can teach us anything." I was told by the husband that if he were the pastor, he would tell the board and people what to do, and not worry if they didn't like what he was doing. That kind of an attitude shows excitement without wisdom, and leads to hurt and discontentment.

This led to all kinds of issues. They eventually moved to another town, but left some hurt and dissention in our church. I truly believe many times this happens because the new ministers are excited about ministry, and want to serve God with all their heart, but have not had mentoring, or have not accepted the mentoring. As leaders we need to provide opportunities for them to grow and learn. As associates we need to make sure we have a teachable, humble spirit, in order to accept the relationship in which God has placed us, with the senior pastor and his wife.

## *Intentional Mentoring*

As senior pastor's wives we need to be the Elijah's to the Elisha's. Are we allowing the Holy Spirit to move upon our heart to pass the mantle to the woman in our care?

As an associate or youth pastor's wife, we need to take advantage of the opportunity to grow, and mature under the leadership of our senior pastor's wife. Learn from her and seek her council. Don't feel like you have to know everything. You can't know everything. You just started in ministry. She is a veteran soldier in God's army. Allow her the opportunity to share what she has learned from the battlefield.

If you are with other women in ministry take time to talk about this. If you are a senior pastor's wife what responsibility do you see yourself having, toward the wives of the associate pastor's in your church? Do you "stay away" in order to not be hurt by them, or do you cultivate a relationship?

If you are an associate's wife what would you like to receive from the senior pastor's wife?

Do either the senior pastor's wives or associate pastor's wives feel threatened by the other one? What can we do to help?

Let this lead into a time of discussion that will ultimately lead to prayer with one another.

If you are meeting with others partner with different women this month. Talk with this woman, find out what has been going on in her life this past month, find out what her prayer needs are and end in a time of prayer. Touch base with each other on a weekly basis via email or the phone. Remember to be transparent and vulnerable with each other, we can not be that way if we do not feel safe with the women we are with.

*My Thoughts and Notes*

## Chapter Three

## God's Gals Called to Serve
*Serve wholeheartedly, as if you were
serving the Lord, not men.*
Galatians 6:7

**Timing is Everything**

David was anointed by God, but lonely and isolated. He was anointed by Samuel to be king, but had to run for his life. Does God anoint us, call us, and let obstacles stand in the way of fulfilling His plan?

What was going through David's mind?

Here he had been anointed by Samuel to be King, but couldn't let anyone know about this anointing. Do you think he felt the anointing was a privilege? We don't know what he thought about that in particular instance, but we do know he did not become angry and bitter.

When something good happens to us don't we want to tell everyone? We can not wait to tell in full detail exactly what happened. David could not do this. Instead, he became a servant.

He played for Saul in order to calm his emotions. (I Sam. 16:21-23)

In everything David did he kept a good spirit. He could have very easily let this affect him negatively, but didn't.

When my husband and I first entered ministry my husband was youth pastor. We were newly weds, so we spent as much time as we could together. It was an exciting new phase in our lives; just out of college, newly married, and our first position as youth pastors. We wanted all our college friends to know we were in a pastoral position and what God was doing in our lives.

David could not do this. He had to come under Saul's authority. He played music for him to calm his spirit. He was in his service.

When expecting your first child you want to tell everyone the minute you find out; but there are times when you must wait, such as in a work environment you need to wait until you absolutely have to let the employer know, or you may have had complications and want to wait a few months before letting people know. This is similar to where David was in his life as anointed king, but unable to say anything.

David was learning to serve.

He was going to have to go through much before he was actually king.

God may plant a desire in your heart many years before He actually allows you to act upon it, or do anything with the desire. You will need to be patient and learn the art of serving. This is very hard to do, because when we know God wants us to do some ministry, our natural inclination is to want to do it immediately. Maybe I am the only one that wants to hurry God, but I don't think so. We get so excited. We have these great ideas. We are motivated to do, but God wants us to wait and learn at His feet first.

I first heard God call me to ministry as a teen. Later, when in ministry, I heard God calling me to various ministries. He would move me from one area into another. That is what is so great about God. You will never be bored if you listen to His calling. It is a great spiritual adventure.

## *People Motivators*

God's calling can evolve as you mature in Him. As a teen I knew God had called me to ministry. My junior high school teacher attended my home church; he encouraged me to become involved in singing. He was an agent God used to help me in my calling. I will never forget Mr. Bettis and his wife.

As women in ministry are we being God's agent motivating and encouraging young people, or young women, in particular, to follow God's call?

In the beginning, I was involved with my husband's ministry; then we began having children. I put most of my efforts into our children, but never stepped completely out of ministry. I volunteered to lead worship and direct Christmas and Easter productions, as well as work with the youth, in the churches in which my husband was pastor.

As the children got older I was able to do more. During these years I felt God planting a desire in my heart for women in ministry. There were certain times in our ministry that I needed a confidant, but could not find her. There were wonderful women in each area we ministered in, but...

*I never had the closeness I needed.*

In those years, the seed was planted to do something to help the woman in ministry develop relationships with other women in ministry. It was not until many years later that that dream actually came into being. I tried several times to make the dream a reality, but it wasn't the right time.

*God has His own timing.*

### *Developing Spiritual Toughness*

God works in our lives through circumstances that come our way in order to spiritually toughen us. This is exactly what David did during the years he was in hiding in the caves. We must learn from his example and make sure we allow the Holy Spirit to mature us, because Satan will try his best to make the circumstances destroy us.

I have a plaque one of our parishioners gave me when I was working as our youth pastor. It reads: "Satan will not continue to assault you if the circumstance he designed to destroy you is now working to perfect you" Author Unknown

There have been many instances in my life in which I had the opportunity to let my faith grow and failed, but there were also those times I did allow God to mature my faith in Him. One of those instances was trusting in Him during our second son's brush with death.

Daniel was only fifteen months old and had been walking since he turned eleven months. He loved cookies and knew exactly where they were in the kitchen. He would go to the kitchen when he wanted a cookie and stomp his feet, point to the cupboard, and say, "cookie, cookie", until we gave him one.

One Saturday morning I had a women's leadership meeting at one of the leader's home. It took me forty-five minutes to get there from where I lived. I looked in on Daniel before I left. He was curled up sucking his thumb. Stan, my husband, and Jonathan, our first son, were outside working on the car. Every few minutes he would check on Daniel.

As soon as I reached the house, where I was going, they told me to call home, because Daniel was not well. I spoke to Stan and knew it was serious. I got back in my car and headed home. When I went to Daniel's bed he was the picture of death. He was staring straight at the ceiling, no thumb in his mouth. I didn't know what to do. I picked him up and started praying in the spirit.

That was all I could do the whole way to the hospital. The nurse immediately took Daniel from me when we walked through the door. Later we found out they had to give him medicine to revive his heart. That thinned his blood out so much he had a stroke on the right side of his brain. The doctors did a spinal tap to test for spinal meningitis and immediately put the antibiotic into his shin bone; that helped the antibiotic start working right away.

They flew him to Children's Hospital of the Kings Daughter's, in Norfolk, from Virginia Beach General. We would follow in our car to the hospital. In all the rush Stan had left the car lights on and when we got to our car the battery was dead. What else was going to go wrong that day?

When we arrived at the hospital we were not allowed to see Daniel. They were working hard trying to keep him alive. All we could do was pray. Later that evening about 9 p.m. we were able to go in and see him. He did have spinal meningitis and homophiles influenza bacteria (HIB). I looked at him. His eyes were open and I began singing "Jesus Loves Me" to him. He closed his eyes, I thought for the night.

The next day I found out he was in a coma that lasted for fifteen days. Six weeks later the neurologist told us Daniel was going home in a semi-comatose state.

During that first night in the hospital I prayed and sought God. I had a dream when I was able to finally fall asleep. I dreamt that Daniel was standing in his bed, stomping his feet, with his head back, laughing from deep within himself. When I awoke I felt that meant Daniel was stomping the devil out of his life. I felt that was my clue that Daniel was going to go home normal.

That was not the case. We took him home and he was not able to focus or see us, he could not talk, he could not walk, he could not use his hands, he could not eat or drink and he could not say cookie anymore.

## *Keeping Faith or Giving Up*

What do you do when your faith has been tested and the outcome is not what you expected?

Do you give up?

Do you forget about believing what the scripture says?

How do you preach healing and restoration when your own son has been affected by disease?

You simply put your trust in God. I knew what the Bible said about healing. I knew that God had given me the word restoration for Daniel. I did not know how or when He was going to heal and restore Daniel, but I knew He could, and the timing was in His hands.

I knew in my spirit that Satan was trying to destroy our ministry by attacking our faith. I was determined that he would not win. From that point on I was going to try to keep our family as normal as possible. We would take Jonathan to his sports activities. When the girls came along we all went everywhere. We did not stop our lives, or ministry, just because we had a handicapped son.

I continued to minister in music and youth. I even became Missionette's Representative and later Women's Ministries Representative, in the Southern Section of the Potomac District of the Assemblies of God.

Satan was not winning this battle.

My faith was strong during that time. We taught our children that one day Daniel would be healed. We told our church that one day Daniel would be healed. Many people have prayed, and are still praying for that healing.

Daniel is now 20 years old and our kids still believe one day he will be restored. God has restored his smile and laugh. Many kids that have a trauma such as his to the brain have to take medicine because they are so irritable. Not Daniel, he is happy and healthier than the rest of us really. He is never sick.

God helped me to toughen my spirit and keep my faith. I was not ready during this time to start a ministry to women in ministry. I was barely doing what I needed to at the time. As a family we all pulled together, but taking care of Daniel fell a lot on me. It would take its toll on me later, along with other issues.

For now I want us to see that God uses circumstances in our lives to prepare us for ministry later. We have to be patient. We have to be faithful to Him. We cannot give up. He will bring those seedlings into full grown plants when it is time.

Where are you right now?

Is God planting seeds in your heart for a ministry he is preparing you for later?

Don't rush the Holy Spirit. Let Him do His work.

Are you at a stage in your life in which God is opening the door and the flower is ready to bloom?

Again, if you are meeting with another woman get with her and share your dreams, share your hurts and sorrows. Is ministry what you thought it would be? Tell her about it. Share from your heart. If you are the woman listening, listen from your heart. Hear the soul of God's Girl next to you. If you are reading this alone use the page provided to write all these thoughts down and then pray them out loud to God.

What is God saying?

Blessings to you, God's Girl!

*My Thoughts and Notes*

## Chapter Four

## God's Gals as Ezer Kenegdo

*"The Lord God said,*
*'It is not good for the man to be alone.*
*I will make a helper suitable for him."*
Genesis 1:18

### Working as a Team

Our marriage relationship is of extreme importance to God. We are going to take a look at Eve and allow God speak to us, through her creation, and what our purpose is in this world as women. There are a few points I am going to make from the book *"Captivating"* by John and Stasi Eldredge.

Let's look at Genesis 1:18, *"The Lord God said, 'It is not good for the man to be alone. I will make a helper suitable for him.'"* Robert Alter is a Hebrew scholar who has translated the book of Genesis. He says this particular passage is extremely difficult because of the word ezer. It is used only 20 other times in the Bible, and each of these times it is referring to God, when He is needed to come through for someone desperately.

Alter says a better translation for the word ezer would be sustainer or lifesaver. He also points out that the commonly used terms for this translation are not the best words that could have been used. He points out that the term "companion" is not the best because today we think of a dog or cat as a companion.

I do not want to be in the same category as my dog!

Another point he brings out is the word "helpmeet" is hard to understand, as a young girl. When you explain this scripture to your daughters they have no idea what helpmeet means.

The next word he translates is kenegdo. This means alongside, opposite, or counterpart. If you put the two words together you could translate it lifesaver alongside.

Gals we are to be a lifesaver alongside our man! The Eldredges also point out that we are to compliment each other. We are not to compete; we are to complete our spouse.

We are not to hide within the image of our spouse. God looked upon creation and was not satisfied. Adam did not even know he was missing anything. He walked with God daily. He had everything he could ever want or need, and yet God said he was not finished.

He knew Adam needed someone to complete him. God created his crowning glory, the finale; woman. They each were going to reflect the other's absence or lack. Together they would be whole. This is true with any male and female relationship. Whether in a work, church, or marriage relationship the male and female have certain qualities they bring, in order to complete and make whole. Men and women are to work along side each other, serving one another, bringing glory to God.

How are we complimenting the men in our lives? As wives what are we doing that is showing we are the lifesaver along side our man? As colleagues in our workplace how are we complimenting those around us? Are we living up to the purpose of our existence as women?

Those are tall questions. When I read and studied other books on the subject it not only freed me in my thinking, but made me feel terrible, because I felt as if I had not lived up to my part of creation. I felt as if I had been working with my husband, and felt as if we were complimenting each other's ministry, but not to the fullest potential.

Stan was blessed with the ability to be patient with seniors and work well with them, while I had more patience with teenagers and worked well with them. But I could have been a better support for him as a wife during difficult times with hurtful people within our congregations.

It took several years for us both to be able to discuss these issues, and understand from the other one's point of view how the other one felt during those stormy times. A practice of extreme importance is that we women must come alongside our husbands and support them with everything within us.

There will be times we do not know what to do, or do not even want to do, because of the circumstances around us at the time. But we must. It is what God desires of each of us. One of the reasons I strongly suggest meeting with other women in ministry, is to form a support for each other, when we feel as if we can't deal with the pressure of the pastorate anymore.

### *Family First*

You will be together to encourage each other as you raise your children. You can share how you have tried to balance the church and family. You will also be able to remind each other that your family does come before the church. I will never forget something that a woman, in church leadership, told me once regarding family. She encouraged moms to go to their child's school function even if it was on a Wednesday night. Let our children see they come before church responsibilities. Do not let the church control you.

That discussion freed me to go to my son's baseball games, or track meets, and not feel guilty. I even became creative and took our youth group to the ball games some of the time. We had a short Bible study that related to baseball before we left and had some great times together. They were able to see that you can be a Christian, participate in outside activities, and be a witness to those people around you.

It can become difficult and overwhelming in our lives, as we raise our children and support our husbands. That is why it is so very important to establish relationships with other women in ministry, in order to encourage and support one another.

Be available for those times when you want to give up. Pray and intercede on each other's behalf. God has started a work in your life so help Him fulfill that work. Satan will try his best to keep us from understanding and realizing the truth behind Gen. 1:18. Don't let him get the best of us.

### *Dangerous Women United*

Prove to Satan you are strong by uniting with a team of women, determined to see God using you, in the way He intended from the beginning of time. As you come to this realization you will become *Dangerous Women* for the kingdom of God.

Lynne Hybels, in her book, *Nice Girls Don't Change the World*, says that dangerous women are those *"who acknowledge our power to change, and grow, and be radically alive for God."* (pg 91) Are you willing to step out of your comfort zone to be the wife your husband needs, and the support other women in ministry need?

**"Let us be the lifesaver alongside our man, encouraging, supporting and loving him the way God desires; in addition to being the lifesaver to other women, who desperately need our support."**

Take the time right now to think of ways you have been a lifesaver to your husband. Write down areas in which you need to improve. I know it will be difficult because no one likes to admit where they have failed, but it will help you become stronger in conquering this part of your life.

If you have been meeting with other women in ministry it will be difficult to admit and share with another person your faults and failures. But if you want to take your relationship with God and each other to another level then this is a must.

Once again a page has been provided for you to write down your thoughts, prayer needs, and praises. My prayer for you is to become a strong, dangerous woman for Christ!

*My Thoughts and Notes*

46

## Chapter Five

## God's Gals and Her Priorities

*"Be very careful then, how you live - not as unwise but as wise, making the most of every opportunity..."*
Ephesians 5:15, 16

### Godly Priorities

After we left our church in Petersburg we moved back to Virginia Beach. I accepted a job for Westminster Canterbury on Chesapeake Bay; which is a retirement community, much like a resort. We found a nice place to rent only three blocks from the beach, and enrolled our kids in school.

We didn't have much money, but we were able to rent in an area where people had money. The girls had friends that were wealthy. The families either had their homes handed down to them by family members, or they were successful businessmen such as doctors and lawyers, etc. When you are around this kind of an atmosphere, you can easily let yourself start wishing you had the money they had, or the jobs they had.

The Bible says to not worry about what you eat or drink because God will provide your needs. When you are around a lot of wealthy people you have to constantly remind yourself of your call and priorities. My husband and I were constantly having to explain to our girls, why they couldn't have everything their friends had. I had to battle against regret and feeling sorry for "poor little ol' us."

I was reminded of something I taught moms many years ago. Be careful to not place your desires, wants, and ministries before your children, husband, and home. When you get those out of whack, you begin to get frustrated, and loose your patience with everyone, yourself included. When you realize the most important thing in your life is your children, not your ministry, you will be much happier.

Like I mentioned in a previous chapter I didn't avoid ministry, I just did not put it as a priority. I did not get as involved in the early years as I did later in the kid's lives. There were times I would have to regroup and remind myself to wait; I would get more involved later, but for the time being I reminded myself to enjoy the kid's while they were young. During Christmas and Easter productions, schedules would become quite hectic, and we all had to learn to let patience rule…that was not always the case.

Those were the times that dinner was usually fast and not as healthy. A lot of the time it was fast food. I would let things go at the house the last week or two before a production. There just didn't seem to be enough time in the day for all I wanted to accomplish.

## *Abishai Congregations*

I remember being encouraged by a woman youth pastor one time at a conference. She mentioned that on Wednesday nights, following a church service a church member would take her kids home when they were younger and get them in bed. I remember wishing someone in our church would volunteer to take my kids.

As I was working with the youth at the time I would try to think of ways to incorporate watching my kids, or helping around my house, into my leadership lessons. It was a good thought on my part, but I didn't do it, because something like that needs to come from the heart. People on a leadership team need to be challenged with examples and then given the opportunity to serve.

Many times our congregations will hear something from someone else, but not from us. Our congregation was never exposed to that way of thinking. Their thought was the pastor's wife had her role as mom and wife. If she chose to do other things along with those responsibilities, she did them on her own. Oh, they let me know that they didn't see how I could do all the things I did, but never offered to help.

Let's look at 1 Sam. 26:5-8, *"Then David set out and went to the place where Saul had camped. He saw where Saul and Abner son of Ner, the commander of the army, had lain down. Saul was lying inside the camp with the army encamped around him. David then asked Ahimelech the Hittite, and Abishai son of Zeruiah, Joab's brother, 'Who will go down into the camp with me to Saul?' 'I'll go with you,' said Abishai. So David and Abishai went to the army by night, and there was Saul, lying asleep inside the camp with his spear stuck in the ground near his head. Abner and the soldiers were lying around him. Abishai said to David, 'Today God has delivered your enemy into your hands. Now let me pin him to the ground with one thrust of my spear; I won't strike him twice.'"*

Abishai was the one who accepted David's challenge to go down to the enemy's camp with him. It was going to be risky, but he was willing to give his life for his leader and friend. I had a young man in our church come up to me, after an evangelist spoke about the relationship of Abishai and David, and say he was going to be my Abishai. He said, "I've got your back Mrs. T." I needed to hear that from him. It was a wonderful word of encouragement for me. He is now the youth pastor at that particular church.

### *Abishai Women*

Let's bring this home to our life. As women we need to be Abishai to our spouse. We need to accept the challenge. Realize ministry is risky. Be willing to stand firm and be the support, the Abishai, your husband needs.

There will be times when we will be hurt by people. It is inevitable. We in turn will unknowingly hurt someone. I have heard it said that if it weren't for the people they would enjoy ministry. That is meant to be a funny statement, yet it is so true. When you work with people you have to learn to live with various personalities. That is tough, but can be rewarding, if you allow.

What are ways you can be an Abishai to your husband?

Are we being an Abishai to our husband or do we need to work on it more?

I want to take this a step further. If you have been meeting with another woman in ministry I want to challenge you to become an Abishai to her. It is my desire to help you and your congregation

I am here for you. I will be glad to minister to the women in your church on leadership and serving from the heart. By doing this I will be able to include examples and ideas of how they can help you in ministry. There are women who have gifts that are not being used to their fullest potential. By helping each woman see the gift she has and sharing ways she can use that gift to help her pastor's family, possibilities of ministry will open she probably never imagined. Think about this for a few minutes – what do you need? How can your congregation be a help to you? If you or your women's ministries invite me to come and minister I will ask you what you need. This will help me help you.

Please, feel free to get with me and schedule a time to come. I am here to help you succeed and flourish in your calling. I want to be an extended Abishai in your life.

Where are you in your life right now?

Do you have children?

Are your children young?

If you are meeting with other women discuss where each of you are in your life and ministry. As you open up glean from one another and take home words of wisdom and guidance. If you are reading this on your own think it through and write it down in your notebook or on the page provided.

*My Thoughts and Notes*

## Chapter Six

## God's Gals Having Fun with Who We Are

*"...I came so they can have real and eternal life, more and better life than they ever dreamed of."*
John 10:10 The Message

### Rekindling Our Passion

God has a desire for us to live. He wants us to enjoy life. If we are not enjoying our lives we need to ask the question, why? We are to be happy in who we are, glad for the opportunity to serve, and delighted for the ability to reach out to hurting and dying people.

In one of our churches many people thought you were a good Christian if you were somber, without much emotion. One of my goals was to help young people understand that living for Christ could be exciting and fun. One of the teenagers used his brother for a science project by having him lie down and relax while he played a slow hymn. He took the pulse of his brother and documented it. He then played a faster, more contemporary song that had rhythm and documented it. He then compared the pulse rate of the two songs. His point was the faster music affected our health in a negative way. It didn't matter if it were Christian music or not. He could not understand the concept of having fun and enjoying his life in Christ. He felt you had to be subdued and serious.

Why would anyone want to have what we have as Christians if we seem to be dull, boring, and lifeless? Do we let ministry and church suck the life out of us? Before we read the scripture I want us to think back to when we were called and first knew God had His hand on our future.

What was that like?

How did you feel? Were you somewhat giddy? Were you excited?

What did you expect?

How were you expecting God to use you? What were the gifts you saw Him using?

How did your personality fit into all He was calling you to do?

Now come back to the present. Do you feel the same way?

Are you still excited and giddy? Are you fulfilling your expectations?

Have you been able to use your gifts? Why or why not?

Has your personality been affected by ministry and in what ways?

If you are meeting with other women in ministry talk about

the differences if there are any. If you are reading this on your own write down the differences.

I Timothy 4:6-18 of *The Message* says, *"You've been raised on the Message of the faith and have followed sound teaching. Now pass on this counsel to the Christians there, and you'll be a good servant of Jesus. Stay clear of silly stories that get dressed up as religion. Exercise daily in God – no spiritual flabbiness, please! Workouts in the gymnasium are useful, but a disciplined life in God is far more so, making you fit both today and forever. You can count on this. Take it to heart. This is why we've thrown ourselves into this venture so totally. We're banking on the living God, Savior of all men and women, especially believers.*

*"Get the word out. Teach all these things. And don't let anyone put you down because you're young. Teach believers with your life by word, by demeanor, by love, by faith, by integrity. Stay at your post reading Scripture, giving counsel, teaching. And that special gift of ministry you were given when the leaders of the church laid hands on you and prayed – keep that dusted off and in use.*

*"Cultivate these things. Immerse yourself in them. The people will all see you mature right before their eyes! Keep a firm grasp on both your character and your teaching. Don't be diverted. Just keep at it. Both you and those who hear you will experience salvation."*

### *Remembering Your Heritage*

Timothy was raised in the faith by his grandmother, Lois, and mother, Eunice. (2 Tim. 1:5) He was fortunate to have this heritage. We all come from a variety of backgrounds. We may not have been as privileged as Timothy. Some of us may have been raised in an abusive home, some from broken, divorced homes, while others may have come from a Christian home much like Timothy's.

Think about this for a minute. What kind of an environment were you raised in? Did you come from a healthy home life? If you are meeting with other women it does help us get to know each other better if we open up and share.

If you were not blessed with a family like Timothy's in which there was the ability to learn about God's goodness as children, thank God for the privilege of learning about Him later in life. Take the opportunity to learn from your past. Teach those around you about the relationship with God you have and help them develop the same relationship.

### *Developing Spiritual Workouts*

In order to teach others properly we need to constantly be in spiritual training. There is much emphasis placed on living healthy and being physically fit. Just think for a minute about the covers of the magazines we see as we are waiting in line at the grocery store. Most all of them talk about health in some way, anything from walking, to how to get our stomach flat. It is almost like we are obsessed with fitness. Some of us adhere to strict regimens while others are defeated before they even start and do not try.

If we were going to go to a trainer for physical training would we go to someone who was overweight and flabby? I don't think so. We would probably look at them and think "why should I trust you? You do not look like you follow your own routine." When we choose a trainer we expect them to follow their own daily or weekly routine as an example for us to follow.

That routine would include focusing on specific areas of our body and doing exercises that focus on a particular muscle.

Why should our spiritual life be different? In actuality it is much more important. We need to evaluate our spirit. What is it we need to work on?

Do we need to work on our attitude?

Have we let church people affect our attitudes and hurt our spirit?

Think about this for a bit. Write down some examples of how you have been affected.

Have you worked through it or are you still trying to work it out?

## *Daily Routine*

Paul tells Timothy to work out daily so he would not become spiritually flabby. It is so important to make sure we do not get so busy doing God's work; we do not allow ourselves to become the woman He desires. What has helped you develop a spiritual routine? Did you have one for a while and then let is fizzle? The very same thing happens with our physical routine. If we stop for a few days, it is so hard to start back up again with the same routine; we were so use to doing.

Is this an area in which you need support through accountability?

What can you do?

Write down some examples.

Find a friend to be your accountability partner.


## Sharing Your Passion

Paul encourages Timothy to pass on what he has learned. Are you able to *"Teach believers with your life by word, by demeanor, by love, by faith, by integrity?"* I hope what you are learning will inspire you to reach out and help other women in ministry. This has been on my heart for years. I know what I needed as a new woman in ministry straight out of Bible College, and didn't feel like I received it. There are too many men and women leaving the ministry because ministry was not what they expected, they were overwhelmed or disillusioned, or they let ministry overtake them and they "lost" their way.

Where are you?

Are you close to getting "lost?"

Are you overwhelmed?

Are you content and happy?

Are you covering up your true feelings?

You will never win if you are not honest and real with yourself.

Paul also told Timothy to keep the special gift he received, when the elders laid their hands on him, dusted off and in use. If you and your husband had a special ceremony, when he was ordained or licensed, think about that for a moment. Wasn't that a special, meaningful time? In our denomination ministers can be ordained after having their license to preach for a certain period of time.

I am only licensed, but my husband is ordained. I remember the ordination ceremony distinctly. One of our executive presbyters prayed for us. This was a very special and stressful time in our lives. Stan's graduation and ordination all took place within a month of each other; and in the middle of this is when Daniel went into the hospital.

Stan had been working on finishing his Master's thesis; in the middle of it is when our son Daniel became critically sick. Stan almost didn't finish his thesis because of all the stress. He did get it finished, and in the acknowledgement section he gives Daniel credit for finishing the book. He stated he was able to finish writing because of Daniel's example. Daniel had a will to fight for his life and live, so how could he not have a will to finish writing and graduate on schedule.

District Council, where Stan was to be ordained, was only three to four weeks after Daniel came out of the hospital. We were not sure we were going to be able to go, because Daniel needed full-time care and it was really impossible to even think about taking him with us. Everything worked out for us to be able to attend. I still remember my dress and the place at the front of the tabernacle where we stood. I remember the mantle being placed on Stan, and the executive presbyter who prayed for us. This was a very special time.

As I read this portion of scripture where Paul tells Timothy to keep the gift dusted and in use I was convicted in my spirit. Paul tells us to cultivate and immerse ourselves in these things. He tells us to keep a firm grasp on our character and our teaching. Don't be diverted. Others will see us mature right before their eyes. Are they seeing us struggle and fall or struggle and grow? This reminds me of a book by John Maxwell called "Failing Forward." Are we learning from our mistakes and the struggles we go through?

Try to be as open and honest as possible with yourself. This is the time you really need to be with another woman in ministry.

By immersing your spirit into God's word you would be able to see how to better cultivate your calling;. If you keep your gifts in use, you are exercising them, not letting them lose tone and shape.

Take a few moments to write down how you are routinely using your gifts. It may be that you have to write down how you are not using your gifts. Be honest with yourself, or you will not benefit from what God wants you to learn. Now, if you feel comfortable, share it with each other; if you are meeting with other women.

*My Thoughts and Notes*

# Chapter Seven

## God's Gals Avoiding Burnout

*"Therefore, since through God's mercy we have this ministry, we do not lose heart...though outwardly we are wasting away, yet inwardly we are being renewed day by day."*
2 Corinthians 4:1 & 16

**The Preciousness of the Call**

As women in ministry we need to understand; ministry has been given to us only through God's mercy. We do not deserve to be ministers; but through His love, mercy, and grace we can be called a woman in ministry.

As stated in our first chapter it is a privilege to be the wife of the pastor, or a woman in ministry. Ministry can be taken from us if we are not careful. We need to realize the preciousness of our calling.

I am reminded of Gollum in *"The Lord of the Rings"* trilogy. The ring was his "precious." It was special to him. He would treat it almost reverently; stroking it ever so gently. Eventually Frodo became "connected" to the ring, becoming possessive. The attachment came between him and his best friend.

Our call into ministry should be that special . . . that precious . . . that sacred. Take ownership of your calling so when Satan or distractions come, you will not give it up easily. You will fight for your calling.

Never take it for granted.

Be careful not to get busy with all the meetings and activities of your calling. When this happens it is easy to neglect time with the Lord. This can come about without even realizing it is happening.

Preparation for a Bible study is not to be a substitute for personal quiet time. They are two totally different disciplines.

Personal quiet time is time alone with God; seeking Him and Him alone.

Prep time for a study is time you spend seeking God alone for others, not yourself. You are seeking God for direction on what to say to others. What He wants to speak through you to them. It is easy to hear what God wants you to tell someone else, and much more difficult to sit quietly and listen to what God desires for you to learn. Those lessons are too close to home. Hearing what God has to say to you personally, may mean you have to change. Many times that is what we do not want to hear.

Do not neglect your personal time. I cannot emphasize it enough.

When difficulties come in life, and personal time with the Lord is neglected, it will be much easier for the devil to get a foothold. Even though scripture has been studied for lessons, Satan will be cunning in his deception. He will use scripture to justify why it is ok to do something, the Bible says is wrong. You know it, but you can justify it; you think.

Satan will be crafty when it comes to ministers and their families. Why? Ministers and their families are tearing down strongholds and destroying Satan's little kingdom. If he can destroy a ministry family he feels he is winning. The more families he can get out of ministry, the better.

## *Standing Against All Odds*

In II Corinthians 4:8, 9, 10 it says, *"We are hard pressed on every side, but not crushed; perplexed, but not in despair; persecuted, but not abandoned; struck down, but not destroyed."* Thank God for these verses. They are so encouraging. Are you getting it? We can feel as if we are the only ones in the world. People in our congregations may be pushing and hitting us with negative words every time we see them. We may even be losing sleep because of it, but the word of God says we will not be crushed, abandoned, or destroyed.

You may have even come to the point of giving up and not caring what happens, to you or your ministry. Be encouraged, you are not alone. God is right there. He will not abandon you. He will not let Satan crush or destroy you.

You may feel as if the life has been crushed out of you.

You may feel as if you are finished in ministry.

THAT IS NOT TRUE.

GOD STILL WANTS YOU.

Those are lies from the depths of hell. God has placed a calling within your heart. That calling cannot be taken away. You can walk away from the calling of God; but GOD WILL NOT TAKE IT FROM YOU.

You make that choice.

Do not let Satan get victory in your life, or your husbands. Do not give up. You may need to take a break from ministry, but the calling is still there, if you choose to accept it.

If you feel as if you are in a place where you are ready to give up on ministry, I want to encourage you to seek council; find a way for you and your husband to take time off for refreshing and rejuvenation. After you and your husband have had a chance to refocus for a couple of weeks, take your family for some much needed time away, from ministry. If finances are a problem I encourage you to let someone know the situation. Find a way to make time away happen.

My husband and I were in a church for ten years. There were many ups and downs during this time. There were times when he was ready to move on and I would encourage him to stay. Then I would be ready to leave and he would encourage me to stay. I believe what we really needed was time away; alone to rejuvenate our personal lives and calling. It took a major crisis to get us to that place.

If you don't feel as if you have these kinds of resources contact me at hstrymknwmn@hotmail.com and I will see what I can do to help.

I am not sure if this will be encouraging or not, but II Corinthians tells us this is all for our benefit; so others may look on us and see God's grace working in our lives. We are living examples of what God can do in others. *"Therefore we do not lose heart. Though outwardly we are wasting away, yet inwardly we are being renewed day by day. For our light and momentary troubles are achieving for us eternal glory that far outweighs them all. So we fix our eyes not on what is seen, but on what is unseen. For what is seen is temporary, but what is unseen is eternal." (II Corinthians 4:16-18)*

Avoiding burnout will be accomplished by adhering to II Corinthians chapter 4.

Keep the calling of God precious in your heart.

Do not let others take that calling from you with words and actions.

Remember you have been called only by the mercy of God.

Next guard your personal private time alone with God. Do not become busy doing and fail to be who God intends you to be.

Find another woman in ministry in whom you can confide and be accountable to in order to guard you own sanity and spiritual growth.

***Staying Focused on Eternity***

Lastly, remember that our eyes are to be set on the things above that are unseen and everlasting. That is so motivating. That is awesome. We are doing things here, in our world that has an eternal impact. It does not matter what others say or do to deter us. Sure, I know it hurts when people in our congregation and circle of influence make negative remarks, but remember your purpose.

God has called you, and He is the one that you will have to stand before, giving an account of how you have followed His instructions. I know it does not ease the pain and hurt caused by others. We are human and we can expect to be hurt if we continue in ministry. But, if we can keep that thought in the forefront of our spirits it will help ease the pain a little.

Partner with someone and discuss where you are in your calling if you are meeting with other women in ministry. If you are reading this alone write down your thoughts.

Where exactly are you right now in your calling?

Are you happy?

Are you satisfied?

Are you feeling neglected and overlooked?

Think about your answers. Pray these answers out loud to God. Tell Him how you feel then let Him speak to you and comfort and encourage your heart. If you are feeling exhausted and disillusioned or disappointed, tell God. You also need to find someone to help you. You are not alone.

After you answer these questions ask yourself these questions...why am I happy...why am I satisfied...why am I feeling neglected...why am I feeling overlooked?

Now, how can you help someone else feel happy and satisfied?

How can you speak encouragement into someone who may feel neglected and overlooked?

If you need some help; again, email me and I will find someone to help. There are resources out there for ministers and their families; we just need to help each other find them.

## My Thoughts and Notes

## Chapter Eight

## God's Gals and Her Man

*"But for Adam no suitable helper was found. So the Lord God caused the man to fall into a deep sleep; and while he was sleeping, he took one of the man's ribs and closed up the place with flesh. Then the Lord God made a woman from the rib he had taken out of the man, and he brought her to the man."*
Genesis 2:20b-22

### *Rekindling the Flame*

Ok. I will admit. This chapter intimidates me because I feel so inadequate. After twenty-six years of marriage I feel as if I am just now getting it when it comes to my man. Even now I feel as if, more often than not, I do it all wrong. I think I will go to my grave wishing I would have done a better job.

I do know this. My husband and I have learned to fall in love with each other and appreciate each other more over the past few years. We are still learning. If we ever get to the point we think "we have arrived" in any area of our life, then we are headed for disaster.

It is so easy to take each other for granted. The more years you are married, the more you need to watch how you act and react to each other. Remember when you first saw that hot guy across the room or down the street, or across the gym? What caught your attention? Use your notebook or the note page at the back of this chapter and write down what caught your attention.

Let's go down memory lane for a few.

Was it his looks? Was it the way he played basketball? Did he play the guitar or sing and he struck a chord in your heart?

Ok. Now think about this. What did you do to get his attention? Did you walk past him twenty million times on the side lines of the gym floor? Did you sit on the front row while he played his guitar and sang? Again, write down your thoughts. It is ok to "remember when." If you are meeting with other women in ministry take time to discuss it with each other. Everyone will enjoy hearing the various experiences. You will all get a laugh out of the stories and how crazy we were…back then.

How long did it take before you got his attention? Did you have to work at it a while? Let me tell you about my experience. I saw my husband to be across the college cafeteria. I thought he was this cool dude from Southern California. I went to school in Missouri and grew up in Oklahoma, so I was use to "cowboy" or "country" dress. This guy had Southern California style and good looks. He was a beach guy, not to be confused with beach bum.

Someone told me he wanted to ask me out. I was excited and was looking forward to him asking me out. I heard he was going to ask me out one weekend. That particular weekend, a guy whom I had wanted to ask me out for several months, asked me to go with him and some friends on a day outing that Saturday. I couldn't believe it. I decided to say no, because I was waiting for Stan (my husband) to ask me out. I told this guy no and Stan never asked me out that weekend!

I found out a friend had come into town and he spent the whole weekend with him. Well, even after that incident, he wasn't asking me out; so a mutual friend tried to arrange something. He set it up so we could all go jogging at a local school track. We all went, but Stan chose to talk, most of the time, to another girl! Can you believe it?

That evening, a girlfriend of mine came to my room, and told me her boyfriend said Stan wanted to go out now for a coke before curfew. She was a true friend; because she got out of bed and went on a double date. Finally, Stan and I got together.

Write your story down in your notebook and take turns telling each other, if you are meeting with other women in ministry. You will all get a laugh, some will cry, and some will be thankful they can even remember.

Now that you have remembered how you and your spouse were brought together; think about how you treated each other. Were you respectful and kind? Did you each go out of your way to do things for the other person? Has that changed over the years? What happened?

### *Unsettling the Unsettledness*

More often than not, we become comfortable with each other, taking each other for granted. Stan and I got to that point. If couples are not aware this could happen, they will let it slip up on them, before they know it. After twenty-two years of marriage, Stan and I came to the realization that we had let ourselves get to that point.

We were thinking more selfishly. Our thoughts and the way we did things were not about the other person, they were more about us. It is also very important, not to let the opinions of congregations, be more important than the opinions of our spouse. Be careful; this can happen unknowingly. Remember, spouses are with us until we die; congregations come and go.

Go the extra mile for your man. This can be hard, when they have done something to hurt us. It is also hard for a strong personality. Remember Ephesians 5:21, *"Submit to one another out of reverence for Christ."* This is easier to accept when we have spent our time with the Lord. When we spend time with God in prayer and reading the word, circumstances do not seem as serious. We can cope better with our everyday routine. Problems will not go away, but we will be able to deal with them better.

Do not forget to show each other how much you love them. Go out of your way to do special things for each other. Do these things, before you get into a crisis. Do not let the busy-ness of ministry crowd out the love, the sensitivity, and friendship you have with your spouse. There are a lot of dos and don'ts in this paragraph, but please listen to this admonishment. It is of utmost importance.

## *Recapturing What is Important*

Couples lose sight of two things and leave the ministry because of them. These two things are: they lose sight of their calling and vision, and they lose sight of their passion and love for each other. How does this happen to two people dedicated to God and each other?

They let doing overshadow being.

I know I have stated this throughout this book, but it is a very important component in staying on track with God.

Pastors are busy doing the work of the pastorate. Some of them remember to be good dads, but neglect being good husbands. Wives are busy being mothers and whatever ministry they have within the church. They can easily be distracted and forget to "woo" their husband to them. Maybe they try, but the husband is too busy with being the pastor that he doesn't notice.

The wife gets discouraged and frustrated and gives up. She then pours all her energy into her children and ministry. She doesn't mean to neglect her husband, but she does. He doesn't realize what he has done. In fact; he thinks he is fine because he is ministering. He is tired at the end of the day and doesn't have time for romance.

One situation leads to another, before long they live in the same house, sleep in the same bed, but are worlds apart. All because they have a calling and they are doing that calling.

Ephesians 5:21 says, *"Submit to one another out of reverence for Christ."* When each one is looking out for the other, not themselves, life is so much easier and less stressful. What would happen if, before you did anything, you would think of how your spouse would react or respond? Would that make a difference in how you made decisions? How would you react or respond if your husband did things with you in mind?

This is difficult to comprehend, because we are in a society that thinks of self above all else. Scripture tells us to think of others above all else. Respect and submission to one another would change marriages, churches and cultures. By submitting to one another it would be so much easier to look at Eph. 5:25 that says, *"Wives, submit to your husbands as to the Lord."* But, it does not say to do it only if our spouse is doing what he should be doing. Too bad. We have to do it no matter what, and that is hard when we feel as if we are not being thought of and treated fairly.

Think about this for a minute; John 15:12-13 says, *"My command is this: Love each other as I have loved you. Greater love has no one than this, that he lay down his life for his friends."* Before anything else our spouse is a child of God. We are to love our spouse as Christ has loved us. He died for us. He called us His friend.

Do we have that kind of love for our spouse? Jesus gave us unconditional love. Can we do that for our man? Is our man our friend? Can we tell him our deepest, innermost thoughts and feelings without feeling we have been rejected? It is my opinion that we need to get to this point in our relationships. This means we are to be vulnerable to each other. No one likes to bear all, be naked, or drop barriers. It is a must if we are to have the relationship God wants us to have.

It is so freeing to be able to open up like this. This is hard to do when you are inundated with ministry. Make it a priority to get away together to get to know each other on a more intimate level. Go away to some remote spot where you will not be bothered with the busyness of others. The best place is in the country, in the mountains, or on a secluded beach.

Rekindle the love you had for one another when you first caught each other's eye. Renew your love, your vision of ministry TOGETHER, and share your hurts, disappointments, and concerns. Discuss your children. Spend time TOGETHER praying and seeking the Lord for direction. Let God move in your lives in ways you have never imagined.

Take time right now to write down where you and your husband are at this time. If you are meeting with other women in ministry, if you feel comfortable, share with each other. Let this be a time of sharing and ministry.

As this chapter ends please understand this is not a comprehensive study on husband and wife relationships. This is not my intent. My purpose was to bring out an area that needs to be guarded with utmost care. Please seek a professional counselor or marriage therapist for more guidance. Like I have stated before if you need help finding a resource contact me at my email address and I will see what I can do to find someone to help.

*My Thoughts and Notes*

## Chapter Nine

## God's Gals in Ministry

*"You did not choose me, but I chose you and appointed you to go and bear fruit - fruit that will last..."*
John 15:16

**Understanding How You Fit**

Where is a woman's place in ministry? In my opinion it is different for every woman. God has created each woman very uniquely. It is to our detriment that we place boundaries on what we can or should do. It is also sad that church culture, as a whole, has placed boundaries on what a woman should do in ministry; particularly the wife of the pastor.

In Chapter Six I touched a little on personalities and gifts. I want to expand on that in light of ministry. God has called each woman to a unique and purposeful ministry. When we start comparing ourselves to other women in ministry; I truly believe God looks at us with a sad heart.

God has called you with a specific purpose in mind; not someone else's purpose. I am speaking to myself also. For many years I would look at other women in ministry and feel sorry for me. I would ask myself questions like, "Why is God allowing her to minister in ways I feel called to minister, and I am not being allowed?" I would ask: "Why? Why? Why?"

That was so wrong. I was allowing negative thoughts to enter into my heart. Those were thoughts, not from God; but Satan. I still catch myself asking the questions and have to remind myself how wrong it is. I believe it disappoints God when we allow our thoughts to follow this path of thinking. We have to learn to be appreciative of where God has placed us for the time being. We may not be ready for that particular ministry at this time in our life.

God is preparing each woman in ministry "for such a time as this." I am reminded of Esther. She could not foresee the future. She did not understand what God was doing, yet she was obedient and did what was expected of her. Come with me on a journey back in time . . .

King Xerxes has just completed years of planning a great expedition to attack Greece. He wants to celebrate the completion of these plans by holding a great celebration. This can be found in the opening chapters of the Book of Esther.

There were many parties and celebrations over the course of several days. Queen Vashti held her own celebration during this time. On one occasion King Xerxes had a bit too much to drink and was in high spirits. He ordered the Queen to come before the men so they could enjoy looking at her.

In all honesty I really do not blame Queen Vashti for not wanting to "flaunt" or parade before all those men. But, that was an order and she was expected to obey. This act of disobedience cost her the title of queen.

Now, isn't it just like a man to change his mind? I am just kidding.

Xerxes did miss Vashti, so it was suggested they search for a new queen. Esther was taken from the familiarity of her home to the palace along with other young women. It was not known that she was Jewish, and Mordecai admonished her not to let anyone know this.

As women in ministry the story should be very familiar. Place yourself in Esther's shoes for a moment. How would you react to being taken from your home? If it were me I would be frightened, and scared to death. Esther had no idea what was going to become of her.

For twelve months she went through a daily regimen of beauty treatments; preparing her to go before the king one time! In today's society I think many women would become bored and rebel. They would "stand up for their rights."

Esther did as she was instructed. Some of us, if in that situation might wonder if our lives were worth much. What would your purpose be? Esther might have become discouraged. We don't really know what went on in her mind and emotions.

### *Staying Focused on Our Purpose*

When God was ready for her to be used she was ready, willing, and sensitive to what God desired of her. She was not side tracked. She did not lose focus. She knew what was needed and trusted God to become real in her life. She could have questioned and complained to Mordecai, but didn't. She did not have a clear understanding of what was happening. She knew enough to have the people pray and fast.

I don't believe our calling is fulfilled overnight. Our purpose may not be revealed to us immediately. If it were we would not have the opportunity to grow and mature into our calling. It should be of major importance to us to continually be sensitive to the Holy Spirit, and God's direction; even when we are unable to see clearly.

Do not question; just innocently trust.

God gradually opens doors to us. We have to understand that He is continually preparing us for His purpose. We have opportunity after opportunity to learn daily, the lessons God gives to us. I would like each woman to ask herself if she is learning. "Am I listening? Do I become impatient and try to open the door on my own?" I, for one, am guilty of rushing God's timing.

I have so much in my spirit I want to share, that I become impatient. On my morning walks I have asked God why He placed such a passion in my heart, for ministry to women, without giving me direction on how to bring ministry about. He quietly reminds me, it is all about Him and His timing; not me and my timing.

So, I continue my walks, my talks, my study and preparation, knowing I am doing what God wants me to do at this time.

One of the lessons we can learn from Esther is; sometimes we do not know why we are being led in a certain direction. We do not understand why God is having us go through phases in our life and ministry. During these phases we may get hurt and become discouraged. Do not lose heart. What we do know, and can see in Esther's life, is God is definitely faithful. He does come through.

There will be struggles in our ministry that we will not understand. We will even get to a point where we wonder if God is even around. Does He see the hurt? Does He understand what we are struggling with? "Are you out there God?" The answer is yes, yes, and yes! He is there, He sees the hurt, and He does understand our struggle. I imagine Esther could have asked the very same questions of God when she found out about Haman's plot.

She had enough discernment and wisdom to ask for the people to fast and pray. They were definitely on her side. Or were they? Let's use our imagination. Were the people really on Esther's side? Did they *all* fast and pray? Maybe some didn't want to. Some may have thought, "How does this beautiful woman know what we should do? Why should we trust her?" We really do not know.

What we do know is God came through for her. She was sensitive to God's will and He used her because of it.

I cannot say that has always been the case for me. It is very disappointing for me to look back in my own life, and see how I allowed circumstances in our church to affect my spirit. Without realizing it anger and bitterness set into my heart. There are leadership messages I taught about being careful of this very thing. Here I was letting it creep inside me!

I allowed people to hurt me and let it harbor in my heart. That is very dangerous. My prayer is that the women reading this book, or listening to my teaching will hear what I learned from experience, and not have to go through what I went through.

Stay away from anger. Find a fellow woman in ministry and do spiritual warfare against the enemy of your soul, who is trying to destroy ministries across this nation and around the world. (II Corinthians 10:3-6)

There are a lot of "I allowed" in this chapter, but that is what happened. I allowed Satan to deceive me about ministry and my family. It felt as if my whole life was ripped away from me. The ministry I felt God had called me to was no longer in my life. I was sitting on the sidelines watching other people do what I felt was my calling, my ministry. My problem was I listened to the lies of Satan; "You are never going to minister again. Your family is better off without you." For a week I left without telling anyone where I was. I didn't care anymore.

God, in His sovereignty took the blinds off my spiritual eyes, and helped me see my family did need me. My husband did love me. God still loved me.

I returned home to a family who accepted me. At that point I was not even sure I wanted to be in ministry. My husband and I had been at our church ten years. We took time off and discussed and prayed about what we should do. We felt it was time to leave. This would allow my husband to work on a Doctorate he had talked about for years, but never found time to do.

Our family packed our things and moved away from the place we had called home for ten years. Our girls left close friends, but we were doing what we felt God was telling us to do. It would take a few years for me to recover. At that point in my life I did not want to be in ministry ever again. I was tired and weary of it all.

Please allow me to be very open and honest with you.

My heart is crying out to women who have been in the trenches, feeling as if the battle is too much.

You may just be starting out in ministry, excited about what God is doing through you.

Some of you may have been in ministry a few years and are becoming disillusioned.

Some may have been in ministry for several years and are ready to quit.

Some may be from small churches; some from large.

It doesn't matter to Satan if you are well known or not, he just wants to kill the heart and life of ministry altogether. Look at what has happened recently with ministers; well known ministers having to readjust their lives. Satan is no respecter of persons.

Now, the vulnerability of my heart – it is resisting somewhat; but, here it goes. At this point in my life; I did not want to step foot in church again. Right after I had to step down from being our youth pastor, I would not walk up the hall; where I had walked to the youth office for years. I went to church on Sundays, went to the sanctuary for service, and went back to the car and left for home. I went because I had to go for my husband. I would use my handicapped son as an excuse some of the time; and not even go to church.

So, when we moved back to Virginia Beach I never wanted to enter a church building again; it reminded me of too much hurt and disappointment. Memories surfaced of how I had been treated. Other women were in front of me leading worship or speaking; these were things I felt called to and they had been taken from me.

For a long time I didn't go. This was a healing time for me. I would pray short prayers and maybe read, but not a lot. Everything I read would remind me of what I could have been teaching. You see, I also felt as if God had abandoned me and allowed my dreams, my ministry, to be taken from me.

You know what? It was not mine to begin with. It was God's.

It took several months for me to actually be able to pray and study the Word again. Gradually I allowed God to whisper to my heart. He never left me . . . I just stopped listening. We were planted in a church where Stan and I, as well as our children were fed and encouraged in our spirit. As we listened to the pastor we began to heal and be restored. Our vision of ministry returned.

All of us, once again, looked forward to being in church. At first I allowed our daughters to be as involved as they wanted and I sat in the congregation as an observer; but when ministry is in your spirit, you can't sit back, you have to be involved. I asked the girls if it was ok if I tried out for the Creative Team.

That was another hurdle I crossed. I led worship. I went to Bible College to learn how to lead. I had attended leadership seminars. I now have to try out for the Creative Team? I did not voice that, but those thoughts crossed my mind and I had to refuse to listen. I made up my mind that it was ok for me to do this. What did I have to worry about anyway? So I became part of the Creative Team. I did not tell anyone what I had done in the past. I just became involved.

God knew my heart and He would bring about His glory in whatever I gave Him to use. As women in ministry we need to be careful that we do not expect things because of who we are…be a servant. Do not go up and tell everyone that you are a minister, just be a person with a heart open to God. You will be amazed at what God will do with that kind of a spirit. Forget titles. Be the PERSON God created you to be.

The ministry to women in ministry God planted in my spirit so many years ago resurfaced. He slowly began developing ideas on how He wanted me to proceed, so I began paying close attention to what He wanted me to do, and when He wanted me to do it. I definitely did not want to go ahead of Him, or be too slow in doing what He was telling me.

As we have seen in Esther's life, God is faithful to us as we listen to Him and discern what He is saying.

Each woman, called by God, has a specific purpose and ministry. Be thankful and grateful for what He has called you to do. Listen attentively to the still, small voice. He loves and cares for each and every woman He calls to ministry; whether in the spotlight or behind the scenes. He will be faithful to what He has called you to do and will give you the willpower and determination you need, just hang in there. (Philippians 1:4)

Do not envy other women in ministry. You are important the way you are. Just like the teachings we teach women in our churches; we are each unique, having gifts God gives us to use, in how He sees fit. I believe that our ministries can change as we mature in Christ. They also change as our children get older. Do not limit God in what He wants to do with you. Come alongside your man in ministry and show Satan who is in charge. Win this battle.

Take some time right now to write in your journal or in the notes provided. Where are you in ministry at this point? Are you anxious because you want to do more than you can at this time in your life? Your children may be young and still need you around more. They may even be teenagers and need you more than ever. Do you feel as if you are being hindered by your church? Does your husband support you in what you desire to do?

I remember a woman youth pastor saying that unless your husband is behind you one hundred percent, you will not succeed. Her husband was the senior pastor. Throughout the years I have seen that to be the case in many instances. You and your husband have to be in this together. He has to believe and support you.

Talk things over with your husband. Let him hear your heart. You both will have to allow God to speak to each of you, especially if some of the ideas are not what each, of you are accustomed to.

After you write your thoughts write a prayer to God. Tell Him how you are feeling. Let Him know of the hurts, the disappointments, the failures. Now that you have written the prayer, sit quietly and let Him speak to you. Do not rush what God wants to do at this time.

Before I end this chapter I want to touch on the thought of bringing our children along with us in ministry. What I mean by this is, if we emulate ministry that is healthy our children will want to "get on board" and be a part of our ministry. If they see a mom and dad who love ministry, but make sure they are giving time to their children they will want what we have.

It is just like sharing the gospel. We want the people who do not know Christ to want what we have, by observing how we live. That is the way we should think of sharing ministry with our children. We want them to want to do ministry by observing how we do ministry.

Now, think of that for a minute and write down your thoughts. How are you and your spouse doing ministry? Are you bringing your children along? Are they observing you and wanting to do ministry with you? Or, are they observing you and saying, "No way. I do not want that life for my family."

Ok. If you are meeting with other women in ministry and feel comfortable sharing, do so at this time. If not I look forward to sharing the last chapter with you celebrating who we are as women called by God.

## My Thoughts and Notes

## Chapter Ten

## God's Gals Celebrating!

*"Though you have not seen Him,
you love Him; and even though
you do not see Him now,
you believe in Him and are
filled with an inexpressible and
glorious joy."*
1 Peter 1:8 NIV

**The Dependent Woman**

Women, you are awesome creations of God! There is a joy you can have because of Christ living in you. Look at what I Peter 1:3-9 of The Message says:

*"What a God we have! And how fortunate we are to have him, this Father of our Master Jesus! Because Jesus was raised from the dead, we've been given a brand-new life and have everything to live for, including a future in heaven – and the future starts now! God is keeping careful watch over us and the future. The Day is coming when you'll have it all – life healed and whole.*

*"I know how great this makes you feel, even though you have to put up with every kind of aggravation in the meantime. Pure*

*gold put in the fire comes out of it proved pure; genuine faith put through this suffering comes out proved genuine. When Jesus wraps this all up, it's your faith, not your gold, that God will have on display as evidence of his victory.*

*"You never saw him, yet you love him. You still don't see him, yet you trust him – with laughter and singing. Because you kept on believing, you'll get what you're looking forward to: total salvation."*

We are women who have Christ in our lives and Peter tells us to greatly rejoice in the NIV version. We should have an inexpressible and glorious joy. This kind of joy only comes through refining. Wait a minute! Peter cannot be telling us the only way to joy is through struggles. How can that be?

Well, I know if you have been in ministry long enough you understand the struggles and conflicts. As I have "matured" in age I have come to realize life is filled with struggles and conflicts. It is a normal way of life. It doesn't matter if you know Christ or not; there is going to be struggles. The difference is in the way the struggles and conflicts are dealt with and handled.

Even believers and those in ministry handle conflicts differently. As women let us determine, at this point in our lives, to deal with the struggles we go through the way God intends. Understand He is there for us. We are not in it alone. He wants us to call out to Him. He doesn't want us to take care of the conflicts alone. He wants us to need Him. He loves helping us.

Women can be very independent; especially in our society. For that reason it is difficult for us to rely totally upon God. We have a tendency to show everyone how we can handle situations on our own. We are independent women. But, God desires us to be totally dependant – upon Him and no one else. Not some of the time – *ALL* OF THE TIME. It is hard for human nature to give in to the spiritual nature; but, it is imperative for this to happen.

Only as we allow our human nature to submit to our spiritual nature will we have true joy and contentment. When we are happy and content everyone around us is happy. It has been said that women are the heartbeat of the home. I believe this. When I am upset I find everything wrong in everyone else. No one is exempt from my "bad moods." I have to really be careful once a month, or God forbid "all hell breaks loose." I am making a conscious effort to help my teenage daughters realize when these once a month occurrences happen in their lives, because God help my husband with three women in the house during this time.

As women we can be happy because of the freedom we have in Christ to live. *"It is for freedom that Christ has set us free..."* (Galatians 5:1 NIV)We can live life to the fullest because of Christ! *"I came so they can have real and eternal life, more and better life than they ever dreamed of."* (John 10:10 The Message) I can think of what I think would be a more and better life. It is quite magnificent. Jesus tells us He came to give us a life greater than we can dream of. Am I living in that better life? To some extent I am living it, but not fully.

What about you? Are you living life to full capacity? What do we, as women, need to change in our lives, right now, to have a better and fuller life? Think about that for a moment. Now write it down in your journal or on the note page provided.

As we come to the end of our time together I want us to think back over the last nine chapters. Where were we, in our lives of ministry, when we first started this journey together? What are some of the lessons we have learned? Have we been able to be open and receptive to what God desires to do in our life? Are we ready to help other women, who are in ministry, live ministry life greater than they have ever dreamed?

Let's spend time sharing with each other and celebrating together! If you have been reading the book on your own, I would love to hear your story of what God has done, while reading.

May God bless you as you continue your journey to a fulfilling life in ministry.

*My Thoughts and Notes*

## Chapter Eleven

## Suggested Reads

The following books are ones I recommend reading. They are each excellent in their own right. I found them to be very encouraging over the years. One of the things I love to do is read, so my list could go for several pages, but I am just including a few at this time. It would be a benefit to you to make the time to read each one.

*High Call; High Privilege* by Gail MacDonald
*Celebration of Discipline* by Richard Foster
*Tale of Three Kings* by Gene Edwards
*Married to a Pastor* by H. B. London and Neil B. Wiseman
*Ordering Your Private World* by Gordon MacDonald
*Wired That Way!* by Marieta Littauer
*Renewal on the Run* by Jill Briscoe
*Wild Goose Chase* by Mark Batterson
*Married for Life* by Jill and Stuart Briscoe

## *About the Author*

Cheryl Turnbull was born in Tulsa, Ok where she lived with her family until attending Central Bible College in Springfield, Mo. After attending CBC for four years, majoring in music, Cheryl married Stanley Turnbull and moved to Virginia Beach, Va. They have lived on the East Coast for the past twenty-five years; in which time, Cheryl received her License to Preach from the Potomac District of the Assemblies of God. During this time she worked as youth pastor and minister of music in the churches in which her husband was pastor. She and her husband have four children, two boys and two girls.

If you would like Cheryl to come and speak for one of your functions she can be contacted via email at hstrymknwmn@hotmail.com or look her up on facebook.com or myspace.com. More information regarding her ministry can be found by visiting her websites: www.mentoringwomeninministry.com and www.mentoringwomeninministry.blogspot.com. Also, look me up on Facebook under Cheryl Turnbull, or Mentoring Women in Ministry Group or Blog.

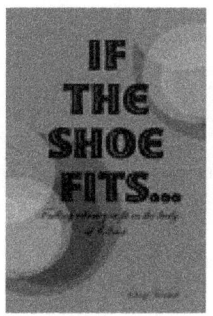

In this book by the author, the reader will be challenged to be all they can be in their life with Christ. She challenges those reading to allow their lives to start bursting with life. Jesus said in John 10:10 of The Message, *"I came so they can have real and eternal life, more and better life than they ever dreamed of."* Are you living up to what God expects of you? Are you enjoying this life you are living?

Order your copy today from www.iftheshoefits.com.

www.ingramcontent.com/pod-product-compliance
Lightning Source LLC
Chambersburg PA
CBHW020013050426
42450CB00005B/448